Chicken Cookbook Recipes

35 Healthy Chicken Recipes for Weight Loss -
Recipe Fried Chicken - Best Healthy Chicken
Recipes and Best Recipes with Chicken

Wanda Carter

ISBN: 9781731034311

Table of Contents

Delicious Honey Garlic Glaze Chicken

Total Time: 30 minutes
Serves: 6 Servings

Ingredients:

- 6 chicken thighs
- 1 tbsp soy sauce
- 2 tbsp rice wine vinegar
- 1/4 cup chicken stock
- 5 tbsp honey
- 5 garlic cloves, crushed
- Parsley, chopped
- Salt

Directions:

1. Season chicken with salt and place in large pan over medium-high heat.
2. Cook chicken on both sides until golden brown. Turn every 5 minutes until done.
3. Once chicken cook then drain excess oil from the pan and leave 2 tbsp of pan juice for flavor.
4. Add crushed garlic between the chicken and stir for 1 minute.
5. Add water, soy sauce, vinegar and honey in pan then increase heat to medium-high and cook until sauce begins to reduce and slightly thicken about 4 minutes.
6. Garnish chicken with chopped parsley.
7. Serve hot chicken with rice and enjoy.

Nutritional Value (Amount per Serving):

- Calories 278
- Fat 8.4 g
- Carbohydrates 15.5 g
- Protein 33.2 g

Easy and Tasty Parmesan Chicken

Total Time: 30 minutes

Serves: 4 Servings

Ingredients:

- 1 lb chicken breasts, skinless and boneless
- 1 egg
- 1/2 cup Parmesan cheese, grated
- 1/2 cup mozzarella cheese, shredded
- 1 cup tomato sauce
- 2 tbsp olive oil
- 1 cup breadcrumbs
- 4 tbsp all purpose flour
- Basil, chopped

- Pepper
- Salt

Directions:

1. Season chicken breasts with pepper and salt and set aside.
2. Add egg in small bowl and whisk well then set aside.
3. Add all purpose flour to shallow dish.
4. Take another dish and mix together Parmesan cheese and breadcrumbs.
5. Take season chicken and dip into the flour then egg and finally coat with breadcrumbs and Parmesan mixture.
6. Add oil in large pan over medium -high heat.
7. Add coated chicken to the hot oil and cook for 3 minutes on each side or until golden brown.
8. Place chicken on the baking tray and top with shredded mozzarella cheese. Broil on high until cheese melted.
9. Top with tomato sauce and garnish with chopped basil.
10. Serve immediately and enjoy.

Nutritional Value (Amount per Serving):

- Calories 451
- Fat 15.7 g
- Carbohydrates 25.8 g
- Protein 38.9 g

- Sugar 4.4 g
- Fiber 2.4 g

Spicy Grilled Chicken

Total Time: 25 minutes

Serves: 4 Servings

Ingredients:

- 2 lbs chicken thighs, skinless and boneless
- 1 tbsp honey
- 2 tbsp red wine vinegar
- 1/2 tsp garlic powder
- 1 tsp thyme
- 1 tsp cumin, ground
- 1 tsp chili powder
- 2 tsp paprika
- 1/2 tsp pepper
- 3/4 tsp salt

- Freshly chopped coriander
- Olive oil, as needed

Directions:

1. Brush grill with oil and preheat to medium-high heat.
2. In a small bowl, mix together pepper, garlic powder, chili powder, cumin, paprika, thyme, and salt.
3. Place chicken in a bowl and sprinkle spice mixture over the chicken.
4. Rub spice mixture over the chicken, make sure chicken is well coated with spice mixture.
5. Grill the chicken 5 minutes per side or until cooked.
6. In a small bowl, mix together honey and red wine vinegar.
7. Brush honey mixture over the grilled chicken.
8. Garnish with chopped coriander. Serve hot and enjoy.

Nutritional Value (Amount per Serving):

- Calories 458
- Fat 16.5 g
- Carbohydrates 6.2 g
- Protein 62.5 g
- Sugar 4.6 g
- Fiber 0.9 g

Tasty Chicken Fried Rice

Total Time: 25 minutes

Serves: 4 Servings

Ingredients:

- 3 chicken breasts, cooked and shredded
- 1 cup rice
- 2 eggs
- 3 tbsp soy sauce
- 3 tbsp olive oil
- 3 carrots, diced
- 1/2 cup frozen peas
- 3 garlic cloves, minced
- 1 medium onion, diced
- Chopped scallions for garnish

Directions:

1. Cook 1 cup rice with 2 cups water in rice cooker.
2. In a large pan add olive oil and heat over the medium heat.
3. Once oil hot then add diced onion, carrots, garlic, and peas. Stir well and cook for 6 minutes.
4. Crack 2 eggs into the pan and scramble with vegetables.
5. Add cooked rice, soy sauce and shredded chicken into the pan. Stir well to combine. Cook for 2 minutes.
6. Remove from heat and garnish with chopped scallions.
7. Serve hot and enjoy.

Nutritional Value (Amount per Serving):

- Calories 347
- Fat 13.1 g
- Carbohydrates 49.0 g
- Protein 8.9 g
- Sugar 4.9 g
- Fiber 3.6 g
- Cholesterol 80 mg

Easy Baked Chicken Nuggets

Total Time: 35 minutes

Serves: 5 Servings

Ingredients:

- 1 lb chicken breast, boneless and skinless
- 1 cup breadcrumbs
- 2 eggs, beaten
- 1 tsp paprika
- 1 cup flour
- Oil for spray
- 1/4 tsp pepper
- 1 tsp salt

Directions:

1. Cut chicken breast into the strips.
2. Preheat the oven at 200 C and spray a baking tray with oil.
3. Take three shallow dishes, in the first dish add flour, pepper, salt, and paprika mix well until combine.
4. Add beaten eggs in a second dish and whisk well.
5. Add breadcrumbs in third shallow dish.
6. Coat chicken strips first with flour mixture then dip into the beaten egg and finally coat with breadcrumbs.
7. Place coated chicken strips on the baking tray and spray with oil.
8. Bake chicken strips into the preheated oven for 20 minutes, flip chicken once halfway through.
9. Serve with tomato sauce and enjoy.

Nutritional Value (Amount per Serving):

- Calories 352
- Fat 6.4 g
- Carbohydrates 35.1 g
- Protein 36.9 g
- Sugar 1.6 g
- Fiber 1.8 g

Chicken with Creamy Mustard Sauce

Total Time: 25 minutes

Serves: 4 Servings

Ingredients:

- 4 chicken breasts, skinless and boneless
- 1/4 cup chicken stock
- 1 tsp oregano, dried
- 2 tbsp Dijon mustard
- 1/2 cup heavy cream
- 2 tbsp olive oil
- Chopped cilantro
- Pepper
- Salt

Directions:

1. Season chicken with pepper and salt. Set aside.
2. Heat olive oil in large pan over the medium-high heat.
3. Add chicken to the pan and sauté until cook, about 10 minutes, flip once.
4. Transfer chicken to a plate and keep warm.
5. Pour chicken stock into the hot pan. Add mustard, oregano, and cream, stir well and cook for about 2 minutes.
6. Pour sauce over the cooked chicken and garnish with chopped cilantro.
7. Serve immediately and enjoy.

Nutritional Value (Amount per Serving):

- Calories 119
- Fat 12.9 g
- Carbohydrates 1.1 g
- Protein 0.7 g
- Cholesterol 20 mg

Crispy and Tasty Chicken Croquettes

Total Time: 1 hour

Serves: 6 Servings

Ingredients:

- 2 cups chicken, cooked and diced
- 1 egg, beaten
- 1 cup breadcrumbs
- 1 tbsp milk
- 1/3 cup flour
- Pinch of pepper
- 1 cup milk
- 4 tbsp butter
- 4 tbsp flour

- 1/2 tsp salt
- Oil

Directions:

1. Melt butter in the pan over medium-low heat, once butter melted then add 4 tbsp flour stir well and cook for 1 minute.
2. Add 1 cup milk and cook over medium heat, stir constantly until thicken.
3. Season with pepper and salt then remove from heat and add cooked chicken. Stir well and place in refrigerator for 1 hour.
4. Shape the chicken mixture into six balls.
5. Mix together egg and 1 tbsp milk, Set aside.
6. Coat chicken croquettes in 1/3 cup flour then dip into the egg mixture and finally coat with breadcrumbs.
7. Fry croquettes in hot oil for 5 minutes or until golden brown.
8. Drain croquettes excess oil on paper towels.
9. Serve with your choice dip and enjoy.

Nutritional Value (Amount per Serving):

- Calories 286
- Fat 11.8 g
- Carbohydrates 24.4 g
- Protein 19.2 g
- Sugar 3.2 g
- Cholesterol 82 mg

Yummy Healthy Chicken Wrap

Total Time: 30 minutes

Serves: 4 Servings

Ingredients:

- 1 lb chicken breasts, skinless and boneless, grilled and chopped
- 4 tbsp sour cream
- 1/2 cup salsa
- 4 whole wheat tortillas
- 1 tsp chili powder
- 1 tbsp lime juice
- 4 tbsp ranch dressing
- 1/2 cup cherry tomatoes, quartered
- 1/2 cup shredded cheese
- 1 cup coleslaw blend

Directions:

1. Preheat the grill to medium heat.
2. In a mixing bowl, mix together grilled chicken, chili powder, lime juice, ranch dressing, cherry tomatoes, shredded cheese and coleslaw blend.
3. Spoon chicken mixture into center of tortillas then fold both sides of tortilla and roll up like burrito style.
4. Grill chicken wrap 8 minutes or until golden brown on both sides. Flip wrap occasionally.
5. Serve chicken wrap topped with sour cream and salsa.

Nutritional Value (Amount per Serving):

- Calories 427
- Fat 16.9 g
- Carbohydrates 26.8 g
- Protein 40.5 g
- Sugar 2.1 g
- Cholesterol 120 mg

Chicken with Vegetables

Total Time: 40 minutes

Serves: 4 Servings

Ingredients:

- 4 chicken breasts, skinless and boneless
- 1/2 lb baby potatoes cut into fourths
- 1 yellow squash, sliced
- 1 zucchini, sliced
- 2 tbsp olive oil
- 1/2 tsp garlic powder
- 1/2 cup Parmesan cheese, grated
- 1/2 cup Italian seasoned breadcrumbs
- 4 tbsp butter, melted
- Pepper

- Salt

Directions:

1. Preheat the oven at 180 C and spray cooking spray in the baking pan.
2. Place melted butter in shallow dish.
3. In another dish mix together Parmesan cheese, breadcrumbs, and garlic powder.
4. Season chicken with pepper and salt then dip into the melted butter and finally coat in Parmesan cheese mixture.
5. Place coated chicken in baking pan.
6. In mixing bowl, add potatoes, yellow squash, zucchini and olive oil toss well. Add some pepper and salt.
7. Place vegetables on sides of chicken in the pan.
8. Bake in preheated oven for 30 minutes or until chicken cooked and vegetables are tender and crispy.
9. Serve hot and enjoy.

Nutritional Value (Amount per Serving):

- Calories 269
- Fat 19.6 g
- Carbohydrates 20.9 g
- Protein 4.9 g
- Sugar 2.7 g
- Cholesterol 30 mg

Easy Cheesy Chicken Rice

Total Time: 35 minutes

Serves: 4 Servings

Ingredients:

- 1 cup chicken breast, cooked and shredded
- 1 cup cheddar cheese, shredded
- 1 cup chicken stock
- 1/2 tbsp fresh thyme, chopped
- 2 tbsp all purpose flour
- 1/2 cup brown rice, cooked, 2 cups after cooking
- 1 tbsp garlic, minced
- 2 tbsp butter
- 1/2 tsp pepper
- 1/1 tsp salt

Directions:

1. Preheat the oven to 180 C.
2. Melt butter in the medium pan over medium-high heat once butter melted then add garlic and cook for 1 minute.
3. Add thyme, pepper, salt and flour stir well.
4. Pour chicken stock into the pan and whisk continuously.
5. Whisk until thick then add cheese and stir until melted.
6. Add chicken and cooked rice stir well to combine. Transfer pan mixture into the baking dish.
7. Top with extra cheddar cheese if you want.
8. Bake for 25 minutes or until cheese is melted.
9. Serve hot and enjoy.

Nutritional Value (Amount per Serving):

- Calories 334
- Fat 17.3 g
- Carbohydrates 22.7 g
- Protein 21.7 g
- Fiber 1.2 g
- Cholesterol 75 mg

Simple and Delicious chicken Pasta

Total Time: 30 minutes

Serves: 6 Servings

Ingredients:

- 1 cup pasta noodles
- 1 1/2 cups shredded chicken
- 1 tbsp ranch seasoning
- 3 cups cheddar cheese, shredded
- 1 1/2 cups milk
- 2 tbsp flour
- 1 tbsp garlic, minced
- 1/2 cup red peppers, diced
- 2 tbsp butter

- Pepper

Directions:

1. Cook pasta noodles according to the package directions. Drain.
2. Melt butter in the large pan once butter melted then add peppers and sauté for 2 minutes.
3. Add flour and garlic in the pan stir well and cook for another 2 minutes.
4. Slowly add milk and cook over medium heat until thicken.
5. Add 2 cups cheese and cook until melted and creamy.
6. Add cooked pasta, ranch seasoning, remaining cheese and chicken stir well to combine. Season with pepper.
7. Serve immediately and enjoy.

Nutritional Value (Amount per Serving):

- Calories 362
- Fat 25.0 g
- Carbohydrates 7.3 g
- Protein 26.8 g
- Sugar 3.7 g
- Cholesterol 100 mg

Hawaiian Style Baked Chicken

Total Time: 1 hour

Serves: 4 Servings

Ingredients:

- 8 chicken thighs
- 1 tsp garlic powder
- 2 tsp sriracha sauce
- 1/4 cup brown sugar
- 1/2 cup soy sauce
- 1 tbsp tomato ketchup
- 2 cups pineapple juice
- 8 pineapple slice
- Freshly chopped coriander

Directions:

1. Preheat the oven to 180 C.
2. In a small pan add pineapple juice, tomato ketchup, soy sauce, brown sugar, sriracha sauce and garlic powder mix well and heat over the medium-high heat about 12 minutes or until thicken.
3. In large baking dish place chicken thighs skin down.
4. Pour pineapple juice mixture over the chicken.
5. Place baking dish in oven and bake for 25 minutes.
6. After 25 minutes flip the chicken and bake for another 20 minutes or until chicken fully cooked.
7. Garnish chicken with chopped coriander.
8. Serve chicken with pineapple slice and enjoy.

Nutritional Value (Amount per Serving):

- Calories 409
- Fat 11.3 g
- Carbohydrates 28.8 g
- Protein 45.2 g
- Fiber 0.6 g
- Cholesterol 130 mg

Creamy Hot Chicken Soup

Total Time: 20 minutes

Serves: 2 Servings

Ingredients:

- 2 cup shredded chicken, cooked
- 1/2 cream cheese
- 1/3 cup hot sauce
- 3 tbsp butter
- 4 cup chicken broth
- 4 tbsp freshly chopped coriander
- Pepper
- Salt

Directions:

1. Add cream cheese, butter, chicken stock and hot sauce in a blender and blend until a smooth puree.
2. Now add this puree in saucepan and cook until it hot does not boil the puree.
3. Then take a serving bowl add hot puree in it. Now add shredded chicken and coriander.
4. Season with pepper and salt as per your taste.
5. Serve hot and enjoy.

Nutritional Value (Amount per Serving):

- Calories 445
- Fat 24.4 g
- Carbohydrates 2.5 g
- Protein 50.2 g
- Sugar 1.9 g
- Cholesterol 145 mg

Baked Rosemary Lemon Chicken

Total Time: 35 minutes

Serves: 2 Servings

Ingredients:

- 2 chicken breasts, boneless and skinless
- 1/2 tbsp olive oil
- 1 lemon juice
- 1 tsp red chili flakes
- 1 garlic clove, minced
- 1 spring rosemary, chopped
- 1 tbsp rosemary leaves
- 12 oz small potatoes, halved
- Salt

Directions:

1. Preheat the oven to 220 C.
2. Cover the potatoes with cold water and salt in a saucepan. Bring to boil potatoes over medium-high heat for 10 minutes. Drain and set aside.
3. In a bowl, place chicken and add spring rosemary, garlic, chili flakes, lemon juice, rosemary leaves and olive oil mix well.
4. In a pan, place chicken over medium-high heat for 5 minutes.
5. Transfer chicken in a baking tray and add potatoes to tray.
6. Place tray in oven and roast chicken for 25 minutes.
7. Serve hot and enjoy.

Nutritional Value (Amount per Serving):

- Calories 435
- Fat 10.1 g
- Carbohydrates 28.3 g
- Sugar 2.0 g
- Protein 54.3 g
- Cholesterol 140 mg

Yummy Wild Rice Chicken Soup

Total Time: 50 minutes

Serves: 6 Servings

Ingredients:

- 4 oz wild rice
- 1/2 cup all-purpose flour
- 2 chicken breasts, cooked and shredded
- 1 bay leaf
- 1/2 tsp dried oregano
- 2 cups milk, divided
- 2 cups water
- 2 can chicken stock
- 3 garlic cloves, minced
- 1 tsp olive oil

- 1 onion, chopped
- 1/2 cup celery, diced
- 1/2 cup carrots, diced
- 1/2 tsp pepper
- Salt

Directions:

1. In a saucepan, add olive oil, onion, carrots and celery and cook for 10 minutes over the medium heat.
2. Then add chicken stock, garlic, water and 1 cup milk in the mixture and mix well.
3. Add oregano, pepper, bay leaf and chicken mix until combine and allow simmering for 15 minutes over medium heat.
4. Mix together 1 cup milk and all-purpose flour and stir in soup mixture and whisk until combined.
5. Add wild rice to soup and simmer for 20 minutes or until rice are cooked.
6. Season soup with pepper and salt to taste.
7. Serve hot and enjoy.

Nutritional Value (Amount per Serving):

- Calories 162
- Fat 2.0 g
- Carbohydrates 29.6 g
- Sugar 5.5 g
- Protein 7.0 g

- Cholesterol 7 mg

Tasty BBQ Chicken Pineapple Wraps

Total Time: 25 minutes

Serves: 4 Servings

Ingredients:

- 4 large wheat tortillas
- 1/4 cup cilantro, chopped
- 1 small onion, chopped
- 2/3 cup fresh pineapple, chopped
- 1/2 cup mozzarella cheese, shredded
- 1/2 cup BBQ sauce
- 2 chicken breasts, skinless and boneless, cut into pieces
- 1 tbsp olive oil
- Pepper

- Salt

Directions:

1. In a pan, heat olive oil over medium heat adds chicken pieces in pan.
2. Season chicken with pepper and salt. Cook chicken until golden brown.
3. Add BBQ sauce in pan and stir well until coated.
4. Place tortilla on plate layer with chicken, pineapple, onion, cheese and cilantro.
5. Roll tortilla and secure with a wooden stick and serve immediately.

Nutritional Value (Amount per Serving):

- Calories 138
- Fat 6.2 g
- Carbohydrates 17.1 g
- Sugar 11.2 g
- Protein 5.0 g
- Cholesterol 8 mg

Healthy Creamy Chicken Stew

Total Time: 1 hour 35 minutes

Serves: 6 Servings

Ingredients:

- 1/2 cup plain yogurt
- 16 oz chicken breasts, skinless and boneless
- 1/3 cup peas
- 1/3 cup corn kernels, frozen
- 1 bay leaf
- 4 cup chicken stock
- 1 tsp dried oregano
- 1 tsp dried thyme
- 1 tsp pepper
- 3 garlic cloves, minced
- 3 carrots, diced
- 3 celery stalks, diced

- 1 onion, diced
- 1 1/2 tsp salt

Directions:

1. Add chicken, onion, carrots, celery, garlic, pepper, oregano, thyme and chicken stock in large pot and stir to combine.
2. Add bay leaf, cover pot with lid and cook over the medium-low heat for 60 minutes or until chicken cook.
3. Remove bay leaf from pot.
4. Remove chicken breast from pot and shred with fork and set aside.
5. Measure out 2 cups liquid from pot and add in blender blend until smooth and return in pot again.
6. Return shredded chicken in pot with peas and yogurt.
7. Recover the pot and cook for 25 minutes.
8. Season with salt and pepper for taste before serving.
9. Serve hot and enjoy.

Nutritional Value (Amount per Serving):

- Calories 204
- Fat 6.4 g
- Carbohydrates 10.7 g
- Sugar 5.1 g
- Protein 24.4 g

- Cholesterol 65 mg

Spicy stuffed chicken Cheese Jalapenos

Total Time: 25 minutes

Serves: 12 Servings

Ingredients:

- 6 jalapenos, halved
- 1/4 tsp garlic powder
- 4 oz cream cheese
- 1/4 tsp dried oregano
- 1/4 cup green onion, sliced
- 1/4 cup Monterrey jack cheese, shredded
- 1/4 tsp dried basil
- 1/2 cup chicken, cooked and shredded
- 1/4 tsp salt

Directions:

1. Preheat the oven to 200 C.
2. Spray a baking tray with cooking spray and set aside.
3. Mix all ingredients in a bowl except jalapenos.
4. Spoon 1 tablespoon mixture into the each halved jalapeno and place stuffed jalapeno on a baking tray.
5. Place baking tray in oven and bake for 25 minutes.
6. Remove from oven let it cool for 5 minutes and serve.

Nutritional Value (Amount per Serving):

- Calories 52
- Fat 4.2 g
- Carbohydrates 0.5 g
- Sugar 0 g
- Protein 3.0 g
- Cholesterol 17 mg

Sweet and Tangy Chicken

Total Time: 30 minutes

Serves: 4 Servings

Ingredients:

- 18 oz chicken breast, skinless and boneless
- 3 tbsp Dijon mustard
- 4 tbsp cup honey
- 3 garlic cloves, minced
- 2 tbsp olive oil
- 1/4 cup parsley, chopped
- Pepper
- Salt

Directions:

1. In a pan, add 1 tbsp olive oil over medium-high heat and place chicken breasts in pan.

2. Season chicken with pepper and salt and cook for 4 minutes each side or until chicken cooked.
3. Remove chicken from pan and set aside.
4. In a small bowl, combine 1 tbsp olive oil, garlic, mustard, and honey.
5. Pour honey mixture over the chicken and place chicken again in the pan. Cook for 3 minutes.
6. Garnish chicken with chopped parsley and serve hot.

Nutritional Value (Amount per Serving):

- Calories 347
- Fat 12.1 g
- Carbohydrates 19.1 g
- Sugar 17.6 g
- Protein 41.8 g
- Cholesterol 102 mg

Chicken Curry with Peanuts

Total Time: 35 minutes

Serves: 6 Servings

Ingredients:

- 1 lb chicken breast sliced
- 1 tbsp curry powder
- 1/2 cup onion
- 6 tbsp coconut oil
- 2 tsp garlic paste
- 2 tsp chopped ginger root
- 15 oz coconut milk
- 4 tbsp roasted peanut
- 1/4 cup chopped cilantro
- Salt

Directions:

1. Heat coconut oil in a pan over medium heat. Add onion and curry powder and sauté until onion are soft.
2. Add sliced chicken and sauté. Now add garlic and ginger and combine well.
3. Then pour coconut milk and water over the chicken add some roasted peanut and mix well.
4. Cook chicken curry about 10 minutes, curry should be thickened and chicken cooked.
5. Now add freshly chopped cilantro and stir well.
6. Serve hot chicken curry with plain rice and enjoy.

Nutritional Value (Amount per Serving):

- Calories 465
- Fat 35.6 g
- Carbohydrates 6.8 g
- Sugar 3.1 g
- Protein 25.4 g
- Cholesterol 65 mg

Hot and Spicy Chicken Wings

Total Time: 35 minutes

Serves: 4 Servings

Ingredients:

- 2 lbs fresh chicken wings
- 1 tbsp brown sugar
- 1 tbsp Worcestershire sauce
- 4 tbsp butter
- 4 tbsp cayenne pepper sauce
- 1 tsp sea salt
- 2 tbsp spring onion, chopped

Directions:

1. Preheat the oven to 180 C and spray the baking tray with oil.

2. Arrange chicken wings on baking tray and place in oven bake for 15 minutes.
3. After 15 minutes toss the wings and change the oven temperature to 200 C and cook for another 15 minutes.
4. In a large mixing bowl mix together brown sugar, Worcestershire sauce, butter, cayenne pepper sauce and salt.
5. Remove wings from oven and place in sauce bowl toss well until all wings are coated well with sauce.
6. Garnish with chopped spring onion.
7. Serve hot and enjoy.

Nutritional Value (Amount per Serving):

- Calories 559
- Fat 29.3 g
- Carbohydrates 5.4 g
- Protein 66.4 g
- Cholesterol 230 mg

Slow Cooker Whole Chicken

Total Time: 4 hour 10 minutes

Serves: 4 Servings

Ingredients:

- 2 lbs whole chicken
- 1/2 tbsp coconut oil
- 1/4 tsp pepper
- 1/4 tsp poultry seasoning
- 1/4 tsp dried thyme
- 1 tsp paprika
- 1/2 tsp salt

Directions:

1. In a small bowl, mix together coconut oil, pepper, poultry seasoning, dried thyme, paprika, and salt.

2. Place a whole chicken in the large dish and rub coconut oil mixture over the chicken.
3. Make sure whole chicken are well coated with seasoning.
4. Place chicken breast side down in the slow cooker and cook on high for 4 hours (165 C).
5. Remove chicken from slow cooker and place on pan. Broil for 3 minutes until chicken skin crisp.
6. Let it cool for 10 minutes before slicing.
7. Serve and enjoy.

Nutritional Value (Amount per Serving):

- Calories 448
- Fat 18.6 g
- Carbohydrates 0.5 g
- Protein 65.7 g
- Cholesterol 202 mg

Grilled BBQ Chicken Drumsticks

Total Time: 35 minutes

Serves: 4 Servings

Ingredients:

- 4 chicken drumsticks
- 1 tbsp olive oil
- 1/4 black pepper
- 1 tsp chili powder
- 2 tsp brown sugar
- 1/2 tbsp mustard
- 2 tbsp ketchup
- 1 garlic clove, minced
- Salt

Directions:

1. Brush grill with oil and preheat to medium-high heat.
2. Add garlic, mustard, ketchup, brown sugar, chili powder, pepper and salt in oil and mix well.
3. Rub the drumstick with marinade and leave to marinate for 20 minutes.
4. Arrange drumstick on hot grill and Cook for 25 minutes. Flip pieces every 5 minutes.
5. Serve hot and enjoy.

Nutritional Value (Amount per Serving):

- Calories 130
- Fat 6.7 g
- Carbohydrates 4.5 g
- Protein 13.3 g
- Cholesterol 38 mg

Delicious Stuffed Chicken Breast

Total Time: 35 minutes

Serves: 2 Servings

Ingredients:

- 2 Chicken breast, boneless
- 1/2 garlic cloves, minced
- 1/4 tomatoes, sliced
- 2 tsp parmesan cheese, grated
- 1 prosciutto slice
- Salsa for serving
- 2 basil leaves
- 1/8 tsp pepper
- Salt

Directions:

1. Preheat the oven to 180 C.
2. Make a cut along the side of the chicken breast to form a pocket.
3. Stuffed each packet with tomato slices, garlic, grated cheese and basil leaves.
4. Cut the prosciutto in half to form 4 equal size pieces.
5. Season the chicken breast with pepper and salt, and wrap each with a slice of prosciutto.
6. Place chicken on baking tray and place in oven. Bake chicken at 200 C for 25 minutes.
7. Serve with salsa and enjoy.

Nutritional Value (Amount per Serving):

- Calories 287
- Fat 6.2 g
- Carbohydrates 0.9 g
- Protein 55.5 g
- Cholesterol 140 mg

Baked Chicken Popcorn

Total Time: 25 minutes

Serves: 4 Servings

Ingredients:

- 1 lb chicken breasts, boneless and skinless, cut into bite-size pieces
- 1/4 cup buttermilk
- 1/4 tsp garlic powder
- 1/4 tsp paprika
- 2 tbsp parmesan cheese, grated
- 2 cups corn flakes
- 1/2 cup flour
- 1 tbsp olive oil
- Pepper
- Salt

Directions:

1. Preheat the oven to 200 C and spray a baking tray with oil. Set aside.
2. Add chicken pieces in a bowl and mix together with garlic powder, pepper, and salt.
3. Add cornflakes, parmesan cheese, pepper, paprika and salt in food processor and process until crumbled.
4. Take two large dishes in one dish place flour.
5. In the second dish add crumbled cornflakes mixture.
6. Add chicken pieces in flour dish and coat well then transfer back to bowl.
7. Drizzle buttermilk over the chicken pieces and mix well.
8. Now place chicken pieces in cornflakes mixture dish and coat well. Make sure all pieces are well coated.
9. Place coated chicken pieces on the baking tray and place in oven. Sprinkle olive oil over the chicken popcorn.
10. Bake chicken popcorn for 15 minutes.
11. Serve hot with sauce and enjoy.

Nutritional Value (Amount per Serving):

- Calories 360
- Fat 12.2 g
- Carbohydrates 25.0 g
- Protein 35.9 g

- Cholesterol 100 mg

Tangy Herb Roasted Chicken

Total Time: 35 minutes

Serves: 2 Servings

Ingredients:

- 1 lb chicken thighs
- 1/8 tsp thyme, dried
- 1/2 tsp fresh rosemary, chopped
- 1 tsp garlic, minced
- 2 tbsp white wine
- 1/2 cup tangerine juice
- 2 tbsp lemon juice
- Black pepper
- Salt

Directions:

1. Place chicken thighs into the bowl.

2. In another bowl, mix together tangerine juice, garlic, white wine, lemon juice, thyme, rosemary, pepper, and salt.
3. Pour bowl mixture over the chicken thighs and place in refrigerator for 20 minutes.
4. Preheat the oven to 230 C and spray a baking tray with oil.
5. After 20 minutes remove chicken from refrigerator and arrange on baking tray place in oven and roast chicken for 25 minutes.
6. Let the chicken cool for 5 minutes before serving.
7. Serve and enjoy.

Nutritional Value (Amount per Serving):

- Calories 473
- Fat 17.0 g
- Carbohydrates 7.4 g
- Sugar 6.0 g
- Protein 66.3 g
- Cholesterol 202 mg

Crispy Chicken Patties

Total Time: 20 minutes

Serves: 6 Servings

Ingredients:

- 2 cups chicken, cooked and shredded
- 2 tbsp olive oil
- 2 tbsp lemon juice
- 4 green onions, chopped
- 1/2 cup crackers, crushed
- 1/3 cup mayonnaise
- Pinch of pepper

Directions:

1. In a bowl, add mayonnaise, crushed crackers, chicken, lemon juice, onion, and pepper mix well until combine.

2. Shape the mixture into the six patties.
3. Heat olive oil in large pan and fry patties over the medium heat for 3 minutes on each side or until golden brown.
4. Serve hot and enjoy.

Nutritional Value (Amount per Serving):

- Calories 192
- Fat 11.8 g
- Carbohydrates 7.1 g
- Sugar 1.3 g
- Protein 14.2 g
- Cholesterol 39 mg

Healthy Chicken Stir Fry

Total Time: 25 minutes

Serves: 4 Servings

Ingredients:

- 1 lb chicken breast, skinless and boneless, cut into pieces
- 2 tsp cornstarch
- 1 1/2 cup broccoli florets
- 2 tsp sugar
- 2 tbsp soy sauce
- 1 cup chicken stock
- 2 tsp ginger, chopped
- 3 garlic cloves, minced
- 1 tbsp olive oil

Directions:

1. Heat olive oil in large pan over the medium-high heat.
2. Add ginger, garlic and chicken into the pan and stir-fry for 3 minutes or until chicken brown.
3. Add 3/4 cup chicken stock, sugar and soy sauce in pan and cover pan with a lid. Cook for 5 minutes, stir twice.
4. Add broccoli flowerets again cover with a lid and cook for another 5 minutes or until broccoli tender and crisp.
5. Mix together cornstarch and remaining chicken stock. Stir in the chicken and cook until sauce is thickened.
6. Serve hot with plain rice and enjoy.

Nutritional Value (Amount per Serving):

- Calories 254
- Fat 7.9 g
- Carbohydrates 7.7 g
- Sugar 3.0 g
- Protein 37.5 g
- Cholesterol 95 mg

Baked Cheesy Chicken Salad

Total Time: 35 minutes

Serves: 5 Servings

Ingredients:

- 1 cup chicken, cubed
- 1/2 cup American cheese, grated
- 1/2 cup mayonnaise
- 1 tbsp lemon juice
- 1/4 tsp salt
- 1 tbsp pimento, diced
- 1 tbsp onion, grated
- 1 tbsp green pepper
- 4 tbsp slivered almonds
- 5 oz frozen green peas
- 1 cup celery, sliced

Directions:

1. Grease a casserole with butter.
2. Combine all ingredients together in a casserole and sprinkle with extra cheese and almond flakes.
3. Place casserole in oven and bake at 180 C for 25 minutes or until cheese is melted.
4. Serve warm and enjoy.

Nutritional Value (Amount per Serving):

- Calories 227
- Fat 14.1 g
- Carbohydrates 12.7 g
- Sugar 4.7 g
- Protein 13.2 g
- Cholesterol 35 mg

Crispy Chicken with Zucchini

Total Time: 25 minutes

Serves: 4 Servings

Ingredients:

- 2 chicken breasts, sliced in half
- 2 garlic cloves, minced
- 1 large zucchini, sliced
- 4 tbsp flour
- 1/2 cup parmesan cheese, grated
- 1/2 cup Italian seasoned breadcrumbs
- 8 tbsp butter, divided

Directions:

1. Melt 2 tbsp butter in large pan over the medium heat.
2. For chicken melt 4 tbsp butter in shallow dish.

3. Take another dish and mix together parmesan cheese, breadcrumbs and flour.
4. Dip chicken into the melted butter then coat with cheese and breadcrumbs mixture and place in pan.
5. Cook chicken about 4 minutes on each side or until cooked and crispy.
6. Transfer chicken on a plate and set aside.
7. Add remaining 2 tbsp of butter to the pan and sauté garlic for 1 minute.
8. Add sliced zucchini in pan and sauté until tender. Season with pepper and salt.
9. Add chicken back into the pan and heat for 1 minute.
10. Serve immediately and enjoy.

Nutritional Value (Amount per Serving):

- Calories 305
- Fat 24.1 g
- Carbohydrates 19.5 g
- Sugar 2.3 g
- Protein 4.2 g
- Cholesterol 60 mg

Simple and Tasty Chicken Cutlet

Total Time: 35 minutes

Serves: 2 Servings

Ingredients:

- 1 chicken breast, skinless and boneless
- 1 egg
- 1/2 cup cheddar cheese, grated
- 1/2 cup breadcrumbs
- 1/2 tsp garlic powder
- 1/4 tsp onion powder
- 1 tbsp water
- 1/4 cup all-purpose flour
- Pepper
- Salt

Directions:

1. Cut chicken breast into two pieces and season with pepper and salt.
2. In a small bowl, beat egg with water and set aside.
3. Mix together breadcrumbs, garlic powder, onion powder and cheese. Add flour in shallow dish.
4. Heat 2 tbsp oil in large frying pan over the medium-high heat.
5. Dip chicken in the flour then in egg and finally coat with breadcrumb mixture.
6. Place coated chicken on hot frying pan and cook about 5 minutes on each side or until golden brown and chicken completely cooked.
7. Serve hot and enjoy.

Nutritional Value (Amount per Serving):

- Calories 454
- Fat 16.2 g
- Carbohydrates 32.7 g
- Sugar 2.3 g
- Protein 42.8 g
- Cholesterol 175 mg

Yummy Chicken Pizza

Total Time: 40 minutes

Serves: 4 Servings

Ingredients:

- 3/4 lb chicken cutlet
- 1 tbsp oregano leaves
- 1 oz parmesan cheese, grated
- 1 cup ricotta cheese
- 1 cup marinara sauce
- 1 lb pizza dough
- 1 tbsp olive oil

Directions:

1. Preheat the oven at 230 C and spray a baking tray with oil. Set aside.

2. Heat olive oil in large pan over medium heat once oil heat place chicken and season with pepper and salt.
3. Cook chicken about 5 minutes on each side. Remove chicken from pan and sliced.
4. Shape pizza dough into four rounds and place on baking tray.
5. Evenly divide top with marinara, ricotta, and chicken. Place tray in oven and bake for 15 minutes or until golden brown.
6. Sprinkle on top parmesan cheese and oregano.
7. Serve warm and enjoy.

Nutritional Value (Amount per Serving):

- Calories 570
- Fat 20.0 g
- Carbohydrates 60.7 g
- Sugar 5.9 g
- Protein 41.6 g
- Cholesterol 80 mg

Chicken Chorizo Tacos

Total Time: 30 minutes

Serves: 2 Servings

Ingredients:

- 2 chicken cutlets, sliced
- 4 tbsp guacamole
- 4 corn tortillas
- 1 tbsp lemon juice
- 1 radish, sliced
- 2 tbsp jicama, sliced
- 1 tsp plus 1/2 tbsp olive oil
- 2 oz chorizo, sliced
- Salt

Directions:

1. In a pan, heat 1 tsp olive oil over the medium heat once oil heat add sliced chorizo and cook for 4 minutes.
2. Add chicken in pan and mix well and cook for 4 minutes. Remove pan from heat and set aside.
3. Mix together radish, jicama, lemon juice and remaining olive oil, Season with salt.
4. Evenly fill tortilla with chicken mixture and slaw.
5. Serve taco with guacamole and enjoy.

Nutritional Value (Amount per Serving):

- Calories 415
- Fat 21.2 g
- Carbohydrates 31.8 g
- Sugar 3.0 g
- Protein 27.5 g
- Cholesterol 65 mg

Quick Chicken Lemon Pasta

Total Time: 25 minutes

Serves: 2 Servings

Ingredients:

- 12 oz penne pasta
- 2 chicken cutlets
- 1 garlic clove, minced
- 2 tbsp olive oil
- 2 tbsp kalamata olives, pitted
- 1 oz pecorino
- 3 tbsp parsley, chopped
- 1/2 tbsp lemon zest
- 1 tbsp lemon juice
- 1/4 lemon, sliced
- Pepper
- Salt

Directions:

1. Cook penne pasta according to the package direction. Drain completely and place in a bowl.
2. In a pan, add chicken with salted water and lemon slice cover pan with lid and cook over medium heat for 5 minutes.
3. Remove chicken from pan and shred with a fork.
4. Add shredded chicken, garlic, olive oil, olives, pecorino, parsley, lemon zest, lemon juice, pepper and salt in pasta bowl.
5. Toss well until combined.
6. Serve immediately and enjoy.

Nutritional Value (Amount per Serving):

- Calories 542
- Fat 17.2 g
- Carbohydrates 64.8 g
- Sugar 4.3 g
- Protein 31.4 g
- Cholesterol 52 mg

Healthy Chicken Salad with Raisins

Total Time: 25 minutes

Serves: 2 Servings

Ingredients:

- 1/2 lb chicken cutlets
- 2 tbsp raisins
- 2 tbsp roasted almonds
- 3 tbsp mayonnaise
- 1/2 shallot, chopped
- 2 stalks celery, chopped
- 1 tbsp celery leaves
- 1/4 lemon sliced
- Pepper
- Salt

Directions:

1. In a pan, add chicken, pepper, salt and lemon with salted water. Cover pan with lid and cook on medium heat for 5 minutes.
2. Remove chicken from pan and shred with a fork. Transfer chicken in mixing bowl.
3. Add chopped celery, shallot, raisins, almonds, mayonnaise in a bowl. Season with pepper.
4. Toss well until combined. Garnish with chopped parsley.
5. Serve immediately and enjoy.

Nutritional Value (Amount per Serving):

- Calories 475
- Fat 36.2 g
- Carbohydrates 11.2 g
- Sugar 6.8 g
- Protein 25.7 g
- Cholesterol 75 mg

The information herein is offered for informational purposes solely and is universal as so. The presentation of the information is without contract or any type of guarantee assurance.

The trademarks that are used are without any consent, and the publication of the trademark is without permission or backing by the trademark owner. All trademarks and brands within this book are for clarifying purposes only and are the owned by the owners themselves, not affiliated with this document.

Made in the USA
Monee, IL
05 November 2020

46753079R00046